HOW DOES
IT GROW?

OAK TREE

by Jinny Johnson

Illustrations by Graham Rosewarne

A⁺

Smart Apple Media

Smart Apple Media
P.O. Box 3263, Mankato, MN 56002

Printed in the United States of America

Library of Congress Cataloging-in-Publication Data

Johnson, Jinny.
  Oak tree / by Jinny Johnson ; illustrations by Graham Rosewarne.
     p. cm. -- (How does it grow?)
  Includes index.
  ISBN 978-1-59920-356-0 (hardcover)
  1. Oak--Growth--Juvenile literature. I. Rosewarne, Graham, ill. II. Title.
  QK495.F14J64 2010
  583'.46--dc22
                                        2009003399

All words in **bold** can be found in the glossary on page 30.

Designed by Helen James
Edited by Mary-Jane Wilkins
Picture research by Su Alexander

Photograph acknowledgements
page 9 George Holland/Photolibrary Group; 19 Richard Packwood/ Photolibrary Group; 25 SGM SGM/Photolibrary Group; 29 Dennis Flahery/Photolibrary Group
Front cover Dennis Flaherty/Photolibrary Group

9 8 7 6 5 4 3 2 1

Contents

A Small Start

Trees are the biggest of all living things, but they start small. A tall oak tree grows from a nut called an **acorn**.

The acorn holds the oak tree's seed. It has a tough shell and it sits in a cup. The cup is attached to the oak branch by a stalk.

Acorns ripen in late summer. They fall from the tree. Inside each acorn is enough food for a tiny tree to start growing.

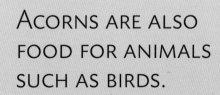

ACORNS ARE ALSO FOOD FOR ANIMALS SUCH AS BIRDS.

How does the seed grow out of the acorn?

Beginning to Grow

The hard shell of the acorn splits
open and a tiny root appears. The
root grows down into the earth
to hold the plant upright.

Next, a stem called a **shoot**
grows up from the acorn
and the first leaves appear.

The leaves of the oak are large
and have toothed edges.

THE SEED SPLITS
OPEN AND THE
ROOT GROWS
OUT OF IT.

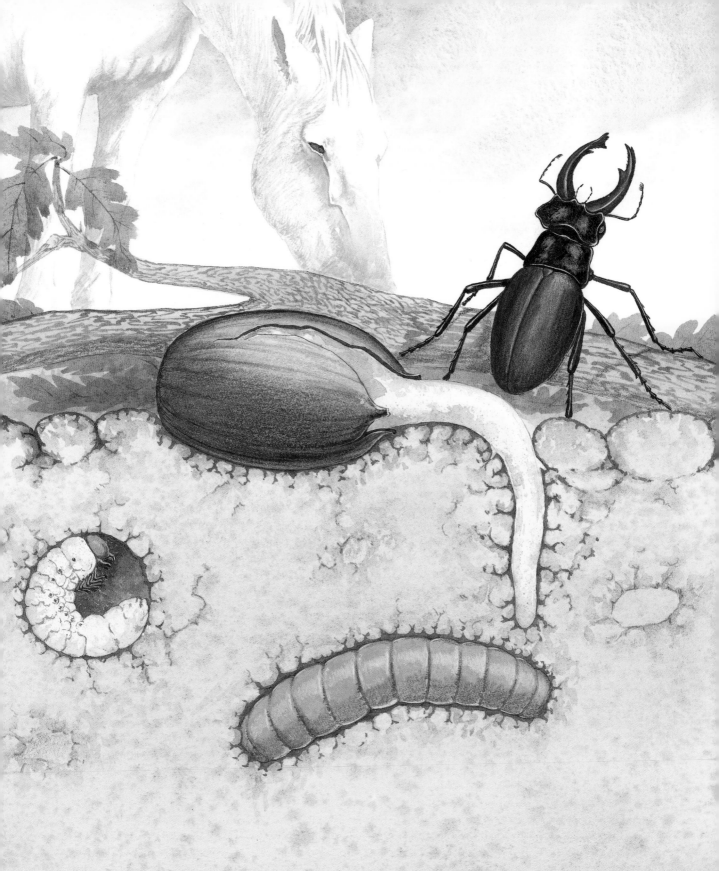

What does the plant need to help it grow?

What the Oak Needs

Like all plants, an oak tree
needs water and sunlight
to help it grow.

Plants make their own food.
The green leaves use water,
sunlight, and a gas called
carbon dioxide in the air
to make their food.

The food helps plants grow
more leaves on their branches
and more roots underground.

THE FIRST LEAVES
TO GROW ARE
VERY TINY.

How long does it take for an oak tree to grow?

Growing Bigger

During its first year, the oak plant grows taller and taller. Many more leaves appear. Its stem is still thin and spindly.

During the second year, the stem starts to grow into a woody **trunk**. It takes about 20 years for an oak to grow from an acorn into a tree.

The tree gets bigger and grows new branches for many more years. Oak trees can live for hundreds of years.

ANIMALS LIKE
TO EXPLORE THE
GROWING OAK TREE.

What is the tree trunk like?

The Tree Trunk

The tree trunk has to be very strong to support all the branches and leaves. As the tree grows, the trunk becomes thicker and thicker.

The tree trunk has a rough covering called **bark**. The bark is like the tree trunk's skin and protects the inside from the weather and damage.

Lots of insects live on the tree trunk. Some are almost the same color so they are very hard to see.

A MOTH BLENDS INTO THE OAK TREE TO HIDE FROM A NEARBY BAT.

What animals live in oak trees?

Home in a Tree

An oak tree is home to lots of creatures. Birds make nests in the branches. Squirrels live in holes in the trunk.

Insects such as butterflies perch on the leaves and beetles scurry around on the bark.

Bigger creatures such as foxes, skunks, and badgers dig dens under the roots of a large tree.

MANY ANIMALS MAKE THEIR HOMES IN OAK TREES.

What happens to the oak tree in autumn?

Autumn

In autumn, the days grow shorter and the weather becomes colder. There is less sunlight to help the tree make food. The leaves change color.

Leaves turn brown or red and begin to fall to the ground. They slowly rot into the earth.

Oak trees lose their leaves so they are protected from the cold. If the leaves stayed on the trees, they could freeze and harm the tree.

THE LEAVES BLOW OFF THE OAK TREE IN BUNCHES, RATHER THAN ALL AT ONCE.

What happens to the tree in the winter?

Winter

In winter, the oak tree's branches are bare. After the leaves fall from the tree in the autumn, the tree rests.

Most of the animals have left the tree, but there may be squirrels taking shelter in holes in the trunk.

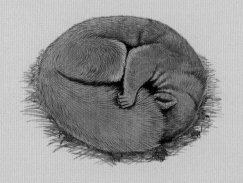

Look carefully and you will see tiny **buds** on the twigs. They are growing bigger, ready to open into new leaves in spring.

THE OAK TREE'S
BRANCHES REMAIN
BARE THROUGH
THE WINTER.

When does the tree grow leaves again?

Spring

The tree wakes from its winter rest in spring. The buds on the oak tree start to open into fresh green leaves.

The days are longer now and there is more sunlight. The leaves can start to make food again.

Birds come back to the tree and start to make nests among the leafy branches.

OAK TREES
PROVIDE SHELTER
FOR NESTING BIRDS
IN THE SPRING.

What else grows on the oak tree?

Oak Flowers

Oak trees grow flowers on them as well as leaves. There are both male and female flowers.

The male flowers are long and straggly and are called **catkins**. The female flowers grow at the tips of the **twigs** and are smaller than the catkins.

The catkins are covered in yellow dust called **pollen**. The pollen is light and blows away in the wind.

When pollen reaches the female flowers, they can make seeds.

BEES ARE DRAWN
TO THE POLLEN ON
THE CATKINS BY THE
POLLEN'S SCENT.

When does the tree grow acorns?

Summer

In summer, the female flowers start to grow into acorns. One part becomes the nut and another part is the acorn cup.

An oak tree doesn't make acorns until it is about 50 years old. Some years an oak might have 50,000 acorns. Other years it has far fewer.

Even when there are thousands of acorns, only a few will grow into oak trees.

ACORNS GROW IN BUNCHES ON THE OAK TREE BRANCH.

What happens to all the acorns?

Starting Again

Birds such as crows and pigeons pick acorns from the branches. Mice, pigs, and deer gobble them up under the tree. Squirrels pick up acorns and hide them away to eat later.

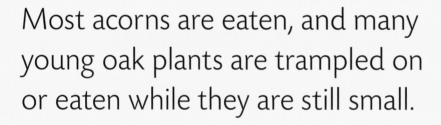

Most acorns are eaten, and many young oak plants are trampled on or eaten while they are still small.

Next spring, one or two acorns will start to grow into big beautiful oak trees, like their parent tree. Eventually they too will grow acorns to make more trees.

ACORNS PROVIDE FOOD FOR DEER AND MICE.

More About Oak Trees

Where do oak trees grow?

There are many different kinds of oak trees. They grow in Europe, Asia, and in both North and South America. Most oaks are deciduous, which means they lose their leaves in autumn and grow new ones that open the following spring. Some oaks are evergreen. Most have leaves with toothed edges.

What do people use oak trees for?

Oak trees provide lots of shade for sitting underneath in warm weather. They are also very strong and sturdy, and make good trees to build tree houses in. When oak trees are cut down, the wood is often used to make furniture.

Where is the oldest living oak tree located?

The Angel Oak is approximately 1,500 years old and is located in the Angel Oak Park in Charleston, South Carolina. The tree is about 65 feet (20 m) high and its **canopy** covers about 17,000 square feet (1,580 square meters).

THIS ALREADY MATURE
OAK TREE MAY LIVE FOR
ANOTHER 100 YEARS.

Words to Remember

acorn
a nut that grows on an oak tree that contains the tree's seeds

bark
the outer covering of a tree's trunk and branches

bud
the part of a plant that grows into a leaf or flower

canopy
a shelter created by a tree's spreading branches and leaves

carbon dioxide
a gas in the air that plants use to make food

catkin
a type of flower that grows on oak trees and some other kinds of trees

pollen
tiny powdery grains made by flowers

shoot
a young plant that has just appeared above the soil

trunk
the woody main stem of a tree

twig
a small branch that may carry leaves, buds, and flowers

Web Sites

For Students
Nature Challenge for Kids
http://www.davidsuzuki.org/kids/

Oak Tree Facts
http://www.oakplus.com/Oak_Tree_Facts.htm

For Teachers
Tree-themed Lesson Plans
http://atozteacherstuff.com/Themes/Trees/

Nature Explore Program for Young Children
http://www.arborday.org/explore/

Index

Withdrawn

**Indianapolis
Marion County
Public Library**

**Renew by Phone
269-5222**

**Renew on the Web
www.imcpl.org**

For General Library Information
please call 269-1700